Cheese and Wine of France

Jean-François Dormoy

GREMESE

Original title: Fromages et Vins de France
Copyright © 1998: Open Door Limited
Translation: Christine Stone

Layout: Mireille Palicot
Photographer: Jean-Paul Paireault
Editor: Dominique Artigaud
Editorial Services: P.E. Fogarty
Editor English Edition: Christine Stone

Photocomposition: IM.A.G.E. - Rome
Printed in Singapore by Imago

Copyright © 1998 GREMESE EDITORE s.r.l.
Via Virginia Agnelli, 88 - 00151 Rome
Fax 39/6/65740509
E-mail: gremese@gremese.com
Internet: www.gremese.com

CONTENTS

INTRODUCTION

Tiny pat or huge wheel, mild aroma or distinctive bouquet, no matter: if it has the makings of a great cheese then so it will be. In all, only thirty-two types have been awarded the Appellation d'Origine Controlée *certificate of genuineness, for it is by observing the requirements of this seal that the precise identity of each cheese has been established. Just as with wines, the* Appellation *in which cheeses are grouped offers gourmets a guarantee of their origin and the certainty of a traditional manufacturing process handed down and refined through the generations. Cheese-making is a precise and sometimes complex ritual that can be traced back to its very origins. It all begins with the coagulation of milk. The curds already form a solid block. For Brie, this needs little working to produce a soft paste, while the hard texture of Comté is obtained by carefully separating, heating and then pressing the curds.*

During the second stage, the draining, the whey is removed to leave just the right proportion of water. The final shape is obtained by forming the cheese in molds of the correct size for each Appellation. *These range from the tiny round disc only a few inches wide used for Picadon to the large wheels of Beaufort. At this point the cheeses are turned and sometimes brushed and washed. This is the skilled technique that gives a reddish hue to the rind of a Maroilles or a Livarot. Knowing how to buy a cheese is the first rule of success. You should therefore learn to exploit the difference between farmhouse cheeses and creamery cheeses. If you want to savor a genuine cheese, then sample the surprisingly unique flavors of farmhouse products. For if France has become the country of great cheeses, she owes it largely to the skill of her farmers. Creamery cheeses, on the other hand, are at their best in cooked dishes. A meal of cheese-based dishes is an original way to pay tribute to your guests. Our recipes instantly acquire the prestige of a long and noble culinary tradition. We all experience the same delight before a dish of* Filets de Sole au Roquefort *and are all captivated by the sophisticated charm of a* Gratin Franc-Comtois. *But, be careful! This originality could whet the appetite for more.*

These cheeses should not be accompanied by just any wine. The combinations of aromas and flavors between wines and cheeses have been a subject of endless controversy among connoisseurs. It is hard to make a rule, but clashes should be avoided at all costs. Obviously, the simplest solution is to capture the particular character of a cheese by accompanying it with a wine from the same area. If you do not want to take a risk, this basic rule gives the best results. But a very happy marriage can also be achieved with other vintages, so long as the tastes are complementary. Since wine and food should enhance not smother each other, we recommend various choices. There are no hard and fast rules in the realm of gastronomy. When marrying two products, the range of wines is great enough to offer a variety of possibilities worth experimenting. It is all a matter of taste and a little curiosity!

CAMEMBERT

- Soft paste with a thin, white velvety crust covered in surface mold, faintly streaked by the large straws on which it is left to ripen.
- Raw cow's milk. It takes 3 ½ pints of milk to make one Camembert.
- 45% fat content.
- Cylinder measuring about 4 ½ inches in diameter and 1 inch high, for a cheese weighing 9 ounces.
- Area of production: Manche, Eure, Calvados, Orne and Seine Maritime.
- Best time: from summer to winter.

At Camembert, a Normandy village in the Orne region, legend has it that a farmer's wife, Marie Harel, was the first person to make this cheese. But as early as 1708, a market used to be held at Vimoutiers where cheeses from Livarot and Camembert were sold.

Since 1880, it has been the custom to package the cheese in a thin wooden box. In the traditional method of manufacture, the curds are molded with a ladle, salted and then dried. Afterwards, the cheese is left to mature in the cellar and turned every forty-eight hours. After ripening for at least twenty-one days, the crust becomes velvety and takes on a faint red hue: the cheese is now ripe.

CRÊPES AU CAMEMBERT
Crêpes with Camembert

PREPARATION TIME: 30 MINS

COOKING TIME: 10 MINS

Prepare the crêpe batter with 1 ¼ cups (5 ounces) flour, 2 ¼ cups (17 fluid ounces) milk, 2 whole eggs, 2 pinches of salt, a sachet/2 ½ level teaspoons of dried yeast.

Remove the crust around the sides of the Camembert.

Leave the crêpe batter to rest and just before using add a good drop of olive oil. Beat vigorously.

Fry the crêpes and keep warm.

Prepare a white sauce and then gradually add the diced Camembert. Cover each crêpe with some of this sauce, then fold in the edges to enclose the filling and make a square shape. Seal the edges with a little beaten egg.

Arrange the crêpes on a lightly buttered oven-proof dish.

Brown gently in a very hot oven and serve while they are soft and creamy.

WHICH WINE?

RASTEAU
POUILLY-VINZELLES
CHIROUBLES

LIVAROT

Produced in a very small area, for a long time Livarot was the best known Normandy cheese. It is even mentioned by Thomas Corneille in his Universal Dictionary of 1708!
The cheese is made exclusively by hand. The milk is curdled, stirred by hand, then molded and finally salted with cooking salt. Twenty-four hours later it is placed in the cellar, where it stays for about a month. The five willow sedges that once bound the sides while it matured have given it the nickname 'colonel'. Today, wood is no longer used, having been replaced by a casing of strips of dark yellow paper or wisps of straw.

- Pliable, elastic paste with a crust tinged any shade of brown.
- Raw cow's milk.
- At least 40% fat content.
- Cylinder measuring about 4 ½ inches in diameter and 2 inches high, weighing around 14 ounces.
- Presented in either a wooden box or unpackaged.
- Area of production: Pays d'Auge, an area straddling the regions of Orne and Calvados.
- Best time: May to December.

GRATINÉE AU LIVAROT
Gratin of Livarot

PREPARATION TIME: 20 MINS

COOKING TIME: 20 MINS

Approximately ¾ pound white onions, 4 ¼ cups (1 ¾ pints) meat broth, 1 glass of dry white wine, half a Livarot, grated Emmental, about half a glass of vermicelli pasta for soup, farmhouse bread.

Finely chop the onions and sauté gently until beginning to brown.
Moisten with the meat broth. Add the vermicelli. Season to taste with salt and pepper and leave to simmer for 20 minutes.
Toast the slices of farmhouse bread. When they have cooled, spread with the Livarot.

Arrange the slices of bread in a soup tureen and cover with the onion soup and white wine.
Sprinkle with a fine layer of grated Emmental.

Place in a very hot oven to brown and serve immediately.

WHICH WINE?

POMMARD
MOULIN À VENT
CORBIÈRES

PONT-L'ÉVÊQUE

- Smooth, grey or yellow to orange crust with a nutty flavor.
- It takes 6 pints of raw cow's milk to make this cheese.
- 45% fat content.
- Square shape measuring 4 ½ inches by 1 inch high. Its weights is close to 13 ounces.
Other shapes include the half and the small Pont-l'Évêque.
- The area of production stretches over the regions of Eure, Manche, Calvados, Orne, Seine-Maritime and Mayenne.
Best time: from the last days of June to the end of March.

WHICH WINE?

MEURSAULT
POMEROL
PINOT D'ALSACE

This cheese was already known in the 13th century under the name Augelot, no doubt derived from the Pays d'Auge area where it is made. In the end it took the name of its village of origin, Pont l'Évêque. In this region, located between Lisieux and Honfleur, it is still possible to find farmhouse cheeses. The curds are stirred by hand and then molded. After draining, the cheese is laid on a mesh, which gives it its wavy appearance. It is then salted before being placed in the cellar to ripen over two to five weeks. Left to ripen dry, it develops a grey rind, veering to yellow if the cheese is washed.

CROÛTES FORESTIÈRES À LA NORMANDE
Country toasts Normandy style

PREPARATION TIME: 10 MINS

COOKING TIME: 20 MINS

Half a Pont-l'Évêque, ½ cup (3 ½ ounces) Normandy butter, 10 ½ ounces mushrooms, 1 cup (7 fluid ounces) thick soured cream (*crème fraîche*), walnut bread, parsley, garlic.

Quarter the tops of the mushrooms and finely chop the stalks.
Fry in a pan until they finish sweating then add a very little garlic and chopped parsley. Season with salt and pepper.
Next add the soured cream and keep warm.

Cut the walnut bread into fairly thick slices and scoop out a little of the center on one side. Brown in the butter.
Garnish with the mushrooms in cream and top with fine strips of Pont-l'Évêque without the crust. Place under the grill for a few minutes.

Serve as soon as the cheese has melted.

11

NEUFCHÂTEL

- A thin, white, velvety crust covered in surface mold tops a pliable and creamy textured paste.
- 45% fat content.
- Characteristics: its many shapes. The weight ranges from 3 ½ ounces (Bonde, Carré or Briquette) to 7 ounces (double Bonde and Coeur).
- The 2.2 pound parallelipiped is less usual.
- Area of production: Seine-Maritime.
- Best time: fall

In matters of cheese-making there can be no doubting the fame of the Pays de Bray. Here Neufchâtel is made, its distant origins going back as far as the 10th century. This cheese is still often found in farmhouse versions, presented on a bed of large straws.
According to tradition, the curds are inoculated by inserting crumbs of a cheese that has already developed mold. The paste is then worked, shaped in a mold and salted. During the two to four weeks it is left to ripen, it gradually develops a velvety white surface and can then be kept for several months. The flavor is at its best when the cheese is made in the area of Neufchâtel-en-Bray.

ENVELOPPÉS DE POIREAUX
Leek rolls

PREPARATION TIME: 10 MINS

COOKING TIME: 30 MINS

WHICH WINE?

SYLVANER
FRONSAC
MOULIN À VENT

Buckwheat pancakes, 5 large leeks, 1 Neufchâtel weighing 3 ½ ounces, 1 cup (7 fluid ounces) thick soured cream (*crème fraîche*), a few leaves of tarragon, ½ cup (3 ½ ounces) unsalted Normandy butter, 1 whole egg beaten.

Use ready-to-cook buckwheat pancakes and fry gently in a skillet with a little unsalted butter. Wash the leeks, cut off the white part and chop finely. Fry in butter over a very gentle flame. When they have finished reducing, add the finely chopped tarragon leaves. Season to taste.
Off the heat, add the soured cream and garnish the center of the buckwheat pancakes with the mixture. Cover with thin slices of Neufchâtel without the rind.
Roll up the pancakes to enclose the filling and fold in the ends. In the same pan, brown the rolls in the remaining butter over a gentle heat.

Serve very hot.

BRIE DE MEAUX

- Soft paste with a crust covered in a soft, velvety white surface mold, often with yellow or golden streaks.
- Flat sphere, 13 ½ inches in diameter and 1 inch high.
- It takes 5 ¾- 6 ¼ gallons of raw cow's milk to make a 5.7 pound cheese.
- 45% fat content.
- Area of production stretching across from the Seine-et-Marne to the Meuse and down from the Marne to the Yonne.
- Best time: from July to March.

According to history it was Charlemagne who discovered Brie de Meaux towards the end of the 8th century. Despite its legendary age, this cheese has never belied its gastronomic reputation. The golden paste, with its fruity flavor, is the result of at least four weeks' slow and gradual ripening, during which the cheese is turned several times by hand. If possible, choose a farmhouse cheese to enjoy fully its delicate nutty flavor.

BOUCHÉES À LA POINTE DE BRIE
Brie vol-au-vents

PREPARATION TIME: 40 MINS

COOKING TIME: 35 MINS

Use bought, ready-cooked vol-au-vent shells, 3 ½ ounce wedge of Brie, 1 ¾ pints mussels, 1 glass of white wine, 7 ounces button mushrooms, 3 ½ ounces cooked and peeled prawns, 3 tablespoons (1 ½ ounces) unsalted butter, 6 tablespoons (1 ½ ounces) flour, garlic, a dash of Madeira.

Steam the mussels open in the white wine with a clove of garlic. Remove from their shells and put aside the liquid. Sweat the chopped mushrooms with a tip of garlic in 1 ½ tablespoons (¾ ounces) of butter. Reserve the liquid.
To make the sauce, melt 1 ½ tablespoons (¾ ounces) butter and stir in the flour. When the mixture froths gradually pour in 2 ¼ cups (17 ½ fluid ounces) liquid reserved from the mushrooms and mussels. Return to a gentle heat for 5 minutes and add the diced wedge of Brie without its crust.
Off the heat, mix together the sauce, mussels, mushrooms, peeled prawns and dash of Madeira.

Fill the heated pastry shells with the sea-food sauce.

WHICH WINE?

MEURSAULT
POMEROL
SANTENAY

BRIE DE MELUN

- Soft paste made with raw cow's milk, the velvety crust bears a slight surface mold, shaded from orange to brown in areas.
- Fat content: at least 45%.
- Flat cylinder smaller in size than Brie de Meaux: 10 ½ inches in diameter, 1 inch high, and weighing 3.3 pounds.
- Area of production: all the Seine-et-Marne region and a small part of Aube and Yonne.
- Best time: from early summer to the end of winter.

For once, all the experts agree that this cheese could well be older than its cousin, Brie de Meaux, but whatever the truth, there is a great difference between the two. The meticulous method of making this cheese is the fruit of long tradition. The period of ripening is slightly longer than that of its cousin, lasting up to seven weeks. It is no doubt this very slow ageing process that gives the cheese its strong bouquet and flavor, heralding a more pronounced character. When cut, always choose the thinner part as the inside is often less ripe where it is thicker.

POMMES DE TERRE BRIARDES
Potatoes with Brie

PREPARATION TIME: 5 MINS

COOKING TIME: 55 MINS

8 large potatoes, ¼ cup (2 ½ ounces) salted butter, 1 cup (7 fluid ounces) thick soured cream (*crème fraîche*), 5 ounces Brie de Melun without the crust, a spoonful of fresh herbs (⅔ chives, ⅓ parsley and tarragon), 5 ounces chopped cooked poultry.

Wash the potatoes and dry carefully.
Wrap in silver foil and cook in a very hot oven for about ¾ of an hour.

Make a lengthways slit in the potatoes. Scoop out part of the pulp and mix well with the other ingredients.
Fill the potatoes with the mixture.

Brown in the oven for 10 minutes and serve.

WHICH WINE?

CROZES-HERMITAGE
CÔTES-DU-RHÔNE
SAUMUR

ÉPOISSES

- Soft paste with a washed, smooth and shiny crust, ranging in color from orange to ochre according to the ripeness.
- Raw cow's milk.
- Very rich: at least 50% fat content.
- 2 shapes: one a disc 4 inches across, the other 7 ½ inches. Both are the same height: between 1 ½ and 2 inches.
- Area of production very limited: part of Haute-Marne, Côte-d'Or and Yonne.
- Best time: this cheese is especially creamy from July to February.

WHICH WINE?

POMMARD
POUILLY-FUISSÉ
MADIRAN

Here is a true Burgundian! Born in the land of Époisses, a village in the Côtes-d'Or region, it is one of the last acid-curd and washed-crust cheeses still made in France. It is washed twice a week over a period of one month with a mixture of white wine and marc (distiller's brandy). It then undergoes a lengthy ripening on rye straw for two months. The result of all this care is a creamy paste with a rich and unforgettable aroma.
This magnificence is no doubt the reason why Brillat-Savarin paid the cheese such extravagant homage!

ÉPOISSES AUX DEUX SALADES
Époisses with two salads

PREPARATION TIME: 10 MINS

Half a 9 ounce Époisses, 3 ½ ounces lamb's lettuce, 3 ½ ounces dandelions, 3 ½ ounces half-shelled walnuts, 2 apples, juice of 1 lemon, parsley and chervil, chives, 2 ½ tablespoons walnut oil, salt and pepper.

Trim the lamb's lettuce and dandelions and wash several times in clean water. Separate the stalks if they are too thick.
Peel and core the apples. Cut them into thin slices and sprinkle with lemon juice to prevent them turning brown. Reserve the juice.
In a salad bowl, mix the salads, the apples, the walnuts and the roughly chopped parsley and chervil.
Dice the Époisses and add to the salad.
Prepare a dressing with the lemon juice and walnut oil. Add salt and freshly ground pepper. Last, add the finely chopped chives.

Pour the dressing over just before serving.

BLEU DE GEX

- Uncooked, veined paste made with whole raw milk, marbled ivory in color and with a firm, ochre crust.
- 50% fat content.
- Flat, wheel weighing around 16 ½ pounds and 4 inches high at the heel.
- Area of production straddling the Ain and the Jura.
- It has three appellations: Bleu de Gex, Bleu du Haut-Jura and Sept-moncel.
- Best time: from August, when the milk is drawn from cows grazing the fields.

WHICH WINE?

ARBOIS-PUPILLIN
MARCILLAC
CORNAS

Legend has it that peasants from Dauphiné who came to live in the region of Gex in 1349 brought with them the tradition of a veined paste. Whatever the truth, the rich milk from the high pastures of the Jura gives this cheese its scented flavor. Rennet is added immediately after milking in mountain huts or creameries and the curds are then salted gradually, giving this cheese its special texture. Three months' ripening in damp cellars allows the blue-green veins to spread evenly. The cheese is unmistakable for since 1935 'GEX' has been stamped in the crust on one side.

SOUFFLÉ AU GEX
Gex soufflé

PREPARATION TIME: 10 MINS

COOKING TIME: 30 MINS

7 ounces Bleu de Gex, ½ cup (3 ½ fluid ounces) thick soured cream (*crème fraîche*), 4 whole eggs, 2 tablespoons (1 ounce) unsalted butter, salt and pepper.

Mix the Gex and the soured cream to a smooth paste with your hands: their heat will be sufficient to soften the cheese.
Separate the eggs and add the yolks to the mixture.
Whisk the whites until they are firm and then fold lightly and gradually into the mixture.
Butter a soufflé dish. Pour in the mixture, smoothing the top with a spatula. Cook in a hot oven.

Serve as soon as the soufflé has risen and turned golden brown.

VACHERIN

To taste this cheese you must wait until the herds return at the beginning of fall. Vacherin, which is still known as Mont-d'Or, is mainly a winter cheese. During that season, its paste is white and creamy and can be eaten on its own with a teaspoon. Savored this way, it is quite delicious.

Ripening begins in the cellar, where the cheese is turned several times and rubbed in brine. After being stocked a further four weeks in the cellar it is at last ready for sale. But beware, there is only very little available.

- Elastic and creamy paste made of raw cow's milk, uncooked, with a pinkish yellow crust, washed and covered in a light surface mold.
- 45% minimum fat content.
- The rounds are always cased in a circle of spruce wood and packaged in a thin wooden box.
- Various sizes, weighing on average 1.5 pounds but rising to as much as 4.4 pounds.
- Area of production: Doubs in the Mont-d'Or region.
- Best time: the period when this cheese is made begins on 15 August and ends punctually on 31 March.

TRÉSOR DU MONT-D'OR
Treasure of Mont-d'Or

PREPARATION TIME: 10 MINS

COOKING TIME: 20 MINS

1 ¼ pounds firm potatoes, 1 Vacherin.

Wash the potatoes carefully and cook them in water.
Peel away the skins, put them on a serving dish and keep warm.
Take the lid off the box of Vacherin, leaving the cheese in the bottom half without removing the hoop of spruce bark.
Place in a very hot oven to warm.
When a golden crust has developed on the surface of the Vacherin, arrange on the serving dish with the potatoes.

The Vacherin is eaten like a fondue, dipping the potatoes into the cheese as a happy alternative to the usual squares of bread.

WHICH WINE?

TROUSSEAU
SAINT-JULIEN
SAVOIE BLANC

COMTÉ

- Pressed and cooked paste made with partially skimmed cow's milk.
- 45% fat content.
- Pale yellow texture, darker in cheeses sold in spring.
- Cylinder 4 inches high and weighing between 88 and 121 pounds.
- Area of production: the regions of Doubs, Jura and the northern part of Ain.
- Best time: in summer the cheeses are fruttiest, while in winter they have a nutty flavor.

It is said that Comté has a tradition going back a thousand years. Many of the dairies that were the forerunners of the present four hundred or so creameries were already producing large wheels of cheese in the 12th century. In keeping with its honourable past, the cheese continues to enjoy the same reputation today. To produce it, the cattle breeders are obliged to join forces because of the huge quantity of milk required. In fact, it takes no less than 132 gallons to make a drum weighing 105 pounds.
Comté will enchant you with its fine, close-textured paste, a source of inexhaustible culinary inspiration.

GRATIN DE COURGETTES
Baby zucchini au gratin

PREPARATION TIME: 10 MINS

COOKING TIME: 30 MINS

WHICH WINE?

ARBOIS VIN JAUNE
MEURSAULT
CAIRANNE

8 fairly small zucchini, 1 cup (7 fluid ounces) thick soured cream (*crème fraîche*), 7 ounces Comté, 2 tablespoons (¾ ounces) unsalted butter, 2 ½ cups (1 pint) white sauce, salt, pepper, nutmeg.

Discard the ends of the zucchini and cut into thin slices.
Fry over a high heat for 20 minutes turning frequently. Arrange in a buttered oven-proof dish.
Grate all the cheese.
Make a white sauce as usual and when nearly ready add 5 ounces of Comté. Remove from the heat and add the soured cream.
Coat the zucchini with this mixture and scatter over the remainder of the Comté.

Brown in the oven for 10 minutes and serve immediately in the same dish.

MUNSTER

- Soft paste made of raw milk from the high stubble fields of Alsace; the washed crust is tinged every shade from yellow to orange.
- Although sometimes flavored with cumin, the natural version is best.
- 45% fat content.
- Great variety of shapes and heights depending on the length of ripening, and a weight ranging from 1 pound to more than 2.2 pounds.
- Area of production extending over the Bas-Rhin, Haut-Rhin, Vosges, Haute-Saône, Meurthe-et-Moselle, Moselle and, last, the Territoire de Belfort.
- Best time: from the beginning of summer to mid-winter, during the period when the cows are at pasture.

WHICH WINE?

JULIENAS
SAINT-CHINIAN

In the 7th century, Irish monks who had settled in the Vosges mountains first began to make a cheese that was given the name Munster. The tradition has been handed down to the present, offering us a paste with a pronounced aroma and exceptional flavor. The curds are first cut and shaped in a mold, then given a lengthy draining. They are salted and afterwards left to ripen slowly in the cellar; during this period they are washed and turned about ten times. The enzymes gradually give the crust its colour, and after several months the cheese reaches full maturity. The farmhouse version, of a pale gold colour, can be trusted to reveal the fullness of its flavor.

PAUPIETTES DE SAUCISSES
Sausage olives

PREPARATION TIME: 10 MINS

COOKING TIME: 10 MINS

6 Frankfurter sausages, 7 ounces Munster, 6 thin slices of raw ham, salt, pepper, mustard, cumin.

Slit the sausages lengthways without separating them completely and spread with mustard.
Fill with a slice of Munster and sprinkle with a little cumin.
Roll each filled sausage in a slice of raw ham and secure with a wooden toothpick.
Arrange on a dish with the cheese filling upwards and place under the grill.

Allow to brown and serve hot as soon as the center begins to darken.

LANGRES

The rich pastures of the region of Haute-Marne have always been renowned as an excellent area for many dairy products, and Bassigny has long been the home of Langres. Indeed, the cheese is already mentioned in texts dating as far back as the 17th century.
It is a very slow-ripening cheese, taking as long as three months to mature. During this time it is washed frequently in brine to obtain a creamy paste, embodying all the subtle flavors of natural meadows. It is also sometimes sold nearly fresh, covered in a white crust.

- Soft paste made from raw cow's milk. The cheese is white when very young, then turns yellow, veering gradually to brown as it ripens.
- Very creamy: at least 50% fat content.
- Cylinder 2 inches high with a slight dip on one of the sides. This can be filled with marc de Bourgogne (Burgundy distiller's brandy) to bring it to perfect ripeness.
- Area of production: Marne, Côte-d'Or and Vosges.
- Best time: produced in the same quality throughout the year, but it is at its best when summer milk is used.

FILET MIGNON
Fillet steak 'mignon'

PREPARATION TIME: 10 MINS

COOKING TIME: 30 MINS

1 ¾ pounds single piece of fillet steak, 4 ounces Langres, 4 ¼ cups (1 ¾ pints) thick soured cream (*crème fraîche*), 4 shallots, ½ glass of dry white wine, 2 tablespoons (1 ounce) butter, salt and pepper.

Melt the butter in a casserole dish and brown the fillet steak on all sides.
Remove the steak. Add the finely chopped shallots to the casserole and then the white wine before replacing the steak. Add salt and pepper, cover and leave to cook gently for 45 minutes.
Meanwhile, remove the crust from the Langres and mix with the soured cream. Season with pepper.
Remove the steak and keep warm. Add the Langres mixture to the casserole and warm for 3 minutes stirring constantly.
Turn the meat in this sauce until completely covered.

Slice the fillet steak and pour over some of the sauce to cover. Serve the remaining sauce separately.

WHICH WINE?

CHAMPAGNE
PULIGNY-MONTRACHET
MORGON

MAROILLES

❦

Maroilles has the fame of being the greatest cheese of northern France. Probably, it is the oldest, for it is said to have been created by the monks of Maroilles Abbey and still retains that name. It is the most powerful, too, exhaling a potent bouquet. After about ten days' drying it develops a surface mold, which is washed in water and beer. This treatment will eventually give the cheese a distinct red colour, similar to that of the typical brick houses of the region. Five weeks' ripening are then needed for the cheese to develop its matchless flavor.

- Soft-paste cheese made from whole raw milk; its crust will develop a velvety white mold before turning a deep reddish brown.
- At least 45% fat content.
- Square measuring 5 inches on each side and 2 ½ inches high. Weight 1 ¾ pounds.
- Area of production: Thiérarche area covering the cantons of Avesne in the Nord region and Vervins in the Aisne.
- Best time: throughout the year, except perhaps spring.

QUICHE AU MAROILLES
Maroilles pie

PREPARATION TIME: 30 MINS

COOKING TIME: 30 MINS

2 cups (7 ounces) flour, ½ cup + 2 tablespoons (5 ounces) unsalted butter, 10 ½ ounces fairly young Maroilles, ½ cup (3 ½ ounces) drained fresh white cheese, 3 whole eggs, salt, pepper, nutmeg.

Make a shortcrust pastry with the flour, ½ cup (3 ½ ounces) butter, 2 pinches of table salt and ½ glass of water.
Leave to rest for 30 minutes then roll out and use to line a pie dish.
Remove the crust from the Maroilles and chop the paste into small cubes.
Beat the eggs, mix in the two cheeses and season lightly with the nutmeg.
Pour this mixture into the pastry base.
Cook for 20 minutes in a medium oven.
Sprinkle over the rest of the butter in knobs and return to the oven for another 10 minutes.

Serve hot with a fresh salad.

❦

WHICH WINE?

SAINT-EMILION
GIGONDAS
CHINON

CHAOURCE

- Soft, white, creamy paste with a crust covered in a velvety, light, white surface mold, left to mature on large straws of rye.
- 50% fat content.
- Two different sizes: the half size and the large, measuring 4 ½ inches across and 2 ½ inches high. The second weighs around 1 pound.
- Area of production: the district covers a small part of Aube and Yonne.
- Best time: like all fat cheeses, the time to choose is when the cheese is made with milk from grazing cows.

Champagne is a generous region. It is well-known for its wines, naturally, but also for giving us Chaource. The label on top of the cheese bears the picture of a cat and a bear, evoking the arms of the town of Chaource, from which it takes its name. It is said that the cheese originated at the same time as the Chablis vineyards, or again that it was invented by the monks of the Abbey of Pontigny, master cheese-makers. Whatever the truth, it continues to be made in the Aube region. The cheese is left to ripen for two weeks on a bed of large rye straw, traces of which can be seen on its delicate crust.

COURGETTES FARCIES
Stuffed zucchini

PREPARATION TIME: 10 MINS

COOKING TIME: 20 MINS

WHICH WINE?

CHAMPAGNE ROSÉ
GEVREY-CHAMBERTIN
PÉCHARMANT

6 small, very young zucchini, 3 ½ ounces of Chaource without the crust, 7 ounces of ham off the bone, 5 ounces Chaource, 3 egg yolks, chives, savory, butter, dried breadcrumbs, salt, pepper.

Blend together well the Chaource and the egg yolks. Add the ham, a tablespoon of chives and a pinch of savory. Season the mix with pepper and a little salt.
Cut the baby zucchini in half, scoop out the flesh and blanch in boiling water. Sprinkle the insides of the zucchini with a little salt and freshly ground pepper. Fill each half with the mixture, cover with a sprinkling of dried breadcrumbs and scatter over a few knobs of butter.

Place in a very hot oven for 10 minutes to brown and serve when the zucchini are soft.

ABONDANCE

- Half-cooked paste made from whole cow's milk, naturally crusted.
- Wheel 16 inches in diameter and up to 26 pounds in weight.
- Over 48% fat content.
- Area of production: pastures in the mountain ranges of Aravis and Mont-Blanc, with a special preference for the Val-d'Abondance.
- Best time: in fall and winter to discover its pleasant and truly full flavor.

Abondance is a rich cheese with a subtle aroma, owing its renown and gastronomic vertues to the particular flora found in natural meadows. These alpine pastures provide grazing for cows of the Abondance breed, which can trace its origins as far back as the 5th century.

Two to three months' maturing, interspersed with regular brushings, gives this cheese its uniquely mild and fruity flavor. It is a slow-ripening cheese, delicious eaten alone, although its fruity aroma also makes it ideal for sauces, gratins or other hot dishes.

ŒUFS BROUILLÉS À L'ABONDANCE
Scrambled eggs with Abondance

PREPARATION TIME: 10 MINS

COOKING TIME: 10 MINS

WHICH WINE?

CHÂTEAU-CHALON
MARGAUX
SAUMUR

8 whole eggs, 3 ½ ounces grated Abondance, 5 tablespoons (2 ½ ounces) butter in knobs, 2 ½ tablespoons thick soured cream (*crème fraîche*), nutmeg, salt, pepper.

Beat the eggs until they are frothy as for an omelette. Season with salt and freshly ground pepper and add just a hint of nutmeg.
Melt the butter in a saucepan placed in hot water on a low boil and then add the mixture.
Continue stirring and gradually add the knobs of butter as the mixture begins to thicken.
When the mixture has become really creamy, add the Abondance and the soured cream, stirring all the time.

Serve immediately.

BEAUFORT

Beaufort is a cheese from the alpine areas of Savoy. It was in the vast expanses of these pastures that the ancient methods of making Beaufort and its lengthy ripening were perfected. Nowadays, the cheese is produced in a uniform and protected mountain region, using biologically pure, whole raw milk.
This is the source of the cheese's fame, for Beaufort draws its flavors from the beautiful flora of the natural high pastures. This prince of cheeses is indeed a noble, gourmet food.

- Fat, firm, elastic and well-flavored paste, almost entirely without holes but with a few thin, horizontal fissures
- It belongs to the category of rich cheeses. At least 50% fat content.
- Presented in the shape of an 88 pound wheel with a flat surface and rounded sides.
- After 6 months' ripening it takes on a colour veering from brown to russet.
- Area of production: Beaufortain, at the foot of the Mont-Blanc, Maurienne and Tarentaise incorporating the Vannoise nature reserve.

TARTE SAVOYARDE AU BEAUFORT
Savoy pie with Beaufort

PREPARATION TIME: 15 MINS

COOKING TIME: 30 MINS

WHICH WINE?

ROUSSETTE DE SAVOIE
CÔTES DE BOURG
SAINT-POURÇAIN

2 cups (7 ounces) flour, ½ cup (3 ½ ounces) butter, half a glass of water, 5 ounces Beaufort, 2 ½ tablespoons thick soured cream (*crème fraîche*), 2 whole eggs, 2 ½ cups (1 pint) whole milk, 1 sachet/2 ½ teaspoons dried yeast, nutmeg, salt, pepper.

Make a shortcrust pastry with the flour, butter, water and 2 large pinches of salt.
Roll out and use to line a buttered pie dish, pricking the base with a fork.
In a bowl, beat the soured cream vigorously with the eggs, the milk and the yeast. Season. Grate in a little nutmeg.
Add the grated Beaufort, beat again, then pour the mixture into the pie shell.
Cook in a hot oven for 30 minutes.

Lift out of the pie dish and serve hot.

REBLOCHON

- Cheese made from whole, raw milk with a lightly pressed, uncooked, salted paste.
- 2 ¼ gallons of milk go in to making 2 Reblochons with at least 45% fat content and each weighing 1 pound.
- Flat cylinder, 5 inches in diameter and 1 ¼ inches high.
- 3 to 4 weeks' ripening.
- Milk from cows of the Abondance, Tarine and Montbéliarde breeds must be used.
- Area of production: Savoie and Haute-Savoie, from Modane to Évian and from Chambéry to Chamonix.
- Best time: finest from June to November.

WHICH WINE?

CÔTES DE FRANC
BROUILLY
MINERVOIS ROSÉ

This is a cheese with a long tradition, for Reblochon first appeared in the 13th century in Haute-Savoie, among the alpine pastures of the limestone Pre-Alps, in the Thônes valley. At that time, a farmer renting an alpine pasture would pay the owner in proportion to the quantity of milk produced. When the landlord came to measure the amount, the farmer would not milk the cows completely. As soon as he left, milking would be completed. This second milking - re-blocher in the local dialect - which was very fat, was immediately used to make the Reblochon. A seal indicates the origin of the cheese: green seal for a farmhouse cheese, red seal for a dairy-farm or creamery product.

TARTIFLETTE
Tartlet

PREPARATION TIME: 20 MINS

COOKING TIME: 40 MINS

2.2 pounds potatoes, cooked, peeled and thinly sliced into rounds, 1 Reblochon with the crust grated by knife, 1 cup (7 fluid ounces) thick soured cream (*crème fraîche*), salt, pepper, garlic, chives.

Line an oven-proof dish with alternating layers of potato rounds and slices of Reblochon, seasoning each time with a little garlic, salt, pepper and chives.
Put in a hot oven for 30 minutes.
Cover with the soured cream and return to the oven for 10 minutes to finish cooking.

Serve hot with smoked cold cuts.

BLEU D'AUVERGNE

- Scented, creamy, veined paste with a natural crust covered in white surface mold.
- Fat content: 50%.
- Presented in the shape of a cylinder between 4 and 8 inches in diameter and 4 inches high.
- Area of production: Cantal, Puy-de-Dôme and part of the Haute-Loire, Aveyron, Corrèze, Lot and Lozère.
- Best time: for farmhouse cheeses, the best times are summer and fall. Otherwise, for creamery produce, the quality is the same all year long.

The silica rich soil of the cold, high plateaus of the Auvergne mountains has destined this land to cattle farming and so to cheese-making, too. Bleu d'Auvergne is a cow's milk cheese, made for the first time in 1845. Its paste is fermented and threaded with molds in fairly close imitation of Roquefort, which is made instead with sheep's milk. The curds are injected with penicillium and pricked with metal needles to help it permeate the cheese. After three months' ripening it acquires an aromatic flavor.

EFFILOCHÉ DE SAUMON AU BLEU
Salmon strips with blue cheese

PREPARATION TIME: 10 MINS

COOKING TIME: 15 MINS

14 ounces tagliatelle pasta, 7 ounces smoked salmon, 4 ½ ounces Bleu d'Auvergne, ½ cup (4 ½ ounces) butter, 1 ⅓ cups (9 fluid ounces) white wine, thick soured cream (crème fraîche), shallots, salt, pepper.

In a high-sided pan, brown the chopped shallots in the butter.
When they have softened, moisten with the white wine and leave to reduce.
Gradually add the diced cheese, sprinkle with a little salt and pepper.
Off the heat, pour in the soured cream and add the smoked salmon cut into strips.

Cook the tagliatelle in plenty of boiling water, drain, add the mixture and serve immediately.

WHICH WINE?

RIESLING
SAUSSIGNAC
GAILLAC ROUGE

CANTAL

- Pressed, uncooked paste, pale yellow in color under a brown rind.
- 45% fat content.
- Cylinder 15 ½ inches in diameter and 17 ½ inches high.
- Area of production: the Cantal district, as well as 44 townships spread around the Puy-de-Dôme, Aveyron, Corrèze and Haute-Loire districts.
- Best time: because of its long ripening time this cheese is available all year round.

In Auvergne, Cantal is known as Fourme, a name derived from the wooden 'form' in which it is kept. To obtain a wheel weighing 110 pounds more than 105.5 gallons of especially rich, scented milk are used, worked according to the traditional methods. The curds are pressed and left to drain. They are then pressed twice again and broken up between each pressing. After forty-five days' ripening a young Cantal with a delicate and lightly scented paste is ready. However, it can be left to mature for up to six months in cold, damp cellars. The cheese will then exhude a full bouquet of fruity aromas.

PAVÉ DE CANTAL
Fried Cantal

PREPARATION TIME: 5 MINS

COOKING TIME: 10 MINS

WHICH WINE?

TAVEL
TRICASTIN
GAILLAC ROSÉ

A large slice of young Cantal weighing 5 ounces, 2 ½ tablespoons (5 ounces) flour, 2 ½ tablespoons olive oil, 1 whole egg, 7 tablespoons fresh breadcrumbs without the crust, salt and pepper.

Take three soup bowls and in the first place the flour, in the second the beaten egg with a spoonful of olive oil, a pinch of salt and some pepper, in the third the breadcrumbs.
Pour a tablespoon of oil into a pan and heat.
Meanwhile, dip the two sides of the Cantal in each of the bowls and then place in the pan.
Brown on both sides, remove and drain quickly on absorbent paper.

Serve immediately while still very hot.

FOURME D'AMBERT

- Fat, veined paste, ivory in color with a few small threads of mold.
- Dry crust covered in surface mold, marked with orange patches and sometimes bearing traces of a fine white down.
- 50% fat content.
- Cylinder measuring about 5 inches in diameter and 8 inches high and weighing 4.4 pounds.
- Area of production: the regions of Loire and Puy-de-Dôme, as well as some districts of Cantal.
- Best time: from summer to winter.

The origins of this Fourme are controversial, some actually maintaining that the cheese goes back a very long way and that no doubt even the ancient Gauls knew of it. It is nevertheless the product of a well-established tradition. The milk used comes from pastures in the high stubble fields of the Monts du Forez, above the passes. The cheese is made in four basic stages: curdling, shaping in the mold, draining and, last, drying. It is pricked with needles before being left to ripen for thirty days so that the paste matures and becomes threaded with blue, acquiring piquancy and a slightly bitter flavor.

TRUITES FARCIES À LA FOURME
Trout stuffed with Fourme

PREPARATION TIME: 20 MINS

COOKING TIME: 10 MINS

4 trout, 1 ounce chopped shallots, 2 glasses of white wine, 10 1/5 ounces Fourme, ½ cup (3 ½ ounces) butter, salt, pepper, thyme, bay leaves.

Scrape off the scales and clean the trout. Wash the inside thoroughly.
In a bowl, mix together the Fourme, the butter and the chopped shallots by hand. Season with pepper and a little salt.
Fill each trout with some of this mixture and sew the sides of the belly tightly together.
Place the trout in an oven dish, pour over the white wine and add the thyme and bay leaves.

Cook in the oven and enjoy.

WHICH WINE?

ENTRE-DEUX-MERS
GIVRY BLANC
JURANÇON

SAINT-NECTAIRE

- Pressed, uncooked paste of an ivory color under a crust covered in brown surface mold.
- 52% fat content.
- Large disc of approximately 8 inches in diameter and 2 inches high, weighing 3 ¾ pounds.
- The seal on the crust is elliptical to indicate farmhouse cheeses and rectangular for creamery.
- Area of production: 72 districts spread over part of the Puy-de-Dôme region and the beginning of Cantal.
- Best time: from summer to winter.

This cheese owes its delicacy and bouquet to the variety of grasses growing in the high pastures of the Dore and Cèzallier mountains, where dairy farming is the principal activity. Whether in the farmhouse or creamery, the method of making this cheese is the same. The cut curds are shaped in a mold and pressed a first time. After draining, the cheese is salted on both sides and put in the press again for twenty-four hours. After this ripening can start. The cheese matures over a period of two months on a bed of rye straw in natural caves formed in the volcanic rock.

SOUPE MITONNÉE AU SAINT-NECTAIRE
Simmered soup with Saint-Nectaire

PREPARATION TIME: **5 MINS**

COOKING TIME: **10 MINS**

1 half-size, very creamy Saint-Nectaire, 3 onions, 5 slices of farmhouse bread, 2 tablespoons (¾ ounces) butter, 1 cup (7 fluid ounces) thick soured cream (*crème fraîche*), 1 ¼ tablespoons chervil, very little salt, pepper.

Fry the slices of bread on both sides in a little butter.
Gently brown the sliced onions in a heavy-bottomed enamel casserole dish, add the bread, some cold water, salt and pepper.
Leave to simmer until the water has reduced.
At this point add the Saint-Nectaire and mix well.

Just before serving, add the soured cream and sprinkly with chervil.

WHICH WINE?

CHIROUBLES
CONDRIEU
FAUGÈRES

- Pressed, uncooked paste made with whole cow's milk. The rind appears slit in places.
- 45% fat content.
- Wheel measuring 20 inches in diameter by 16 inches high. Weight 110 pounds.
- Area of production: the whole of the Cantal region as well as the cantons bordering Aveyron, Puy-de-Dôme, Corrèze and Haute-Loire.
- Best time: available all year round, but best after a lengthy ripening.

WHICH WINE?

CÔTES DU FOREZ
CONDRIEU

SALERS

Salers, it is said, has a very ancient tradition. Many of the high mountain huts that give temporary shelter to herdsmen during the 'summer' period stretching from 31 May to the end of October, have long been the most propitious place to make this cheese. The methods used to produce Salers are exactly the same as for Cantal. After being twice pressed, it is also brushed so that the crust becomes thick and grey. It is a cheese for the larder, maturing over a period of three months to one year. It will then be ready to captivate even the most demanding palates.

GRATINÉE DE POULET
Chicken gratin

PREPARATION TIME: 10 MINS

COOKING TIME: 45 MINS

4 chicken legs, 7 ounces Salers, 2 ½ tablespoons of olive oil, ¼ cup (1 ounce) flour, 2 tablespoons (¾ ounces) butter, 1 ¾ cups (14 fluid ounces) chicken broth, 1 egg yolk, 1 shallot, 3 tablespoons thick soured cream (*crème fraîche*), 3 large pinches of fresh tarragon, pepper.

Brown the chicken legs in very hot oil in a high-sided pan. Add the chicken broth, the shallot and the tarragon. Season with pepper, cover and leave to simmer for 30 minutes without allowing the liquid to reduce too much.
In a saucepan, make a roux with the flour and butter. Off the heat, pour in the cooking liquid from the chicken. Return to a gentle heat, stirring frequently.
Thicken the sauce with the egg yolk, the soured cream and then half the cheese, which you have grated beforehand.
Arrange the chicken in an oven-proof dish and cover with the sauce.

Sprinkle with the remainder of the cheese and brown for 10 minutes.

LAGUIOLE

- Pale golden yellow, uncooked, pressed paste. Thick brown rind.
- Milk collected from farms located at over 2624 feet must be used.
- 45% fat content.
- Cylinder with a slightly rounded heel, weighing around 101 pounds.
- Area of production: 48 districts in the Cantal, Aveyron and Lozère regions.
- Best time: all year round. Its authenticity is guaranteed by the bull stamped on one of the sides

The village of Laguiole used to lie along the pilgrims' route from Puy en Velay to Compostela. As early as 1120, the first Dômerie d'Aubrac was established on its land, offering the pilgrims a reliable asylum for centuries after. All this would be just historical background were it not for the fact that this monastery-hospice gave birth to the great cheese-making tradition of Laguiole. To produce this cheese, rennet is added to raw, whole milk. The curds that are obtained are then pressed in blocks: the tommes. *These are salted together and left to ripen slowly in cellars for at least four months.*
As the cheese ages, the rind becomes thicker and darker.

L'ALIGOT
Aligot

PREPARATION TIME: 15 MINS

COOKING TIME: 45 MINS

2.2 pounds Bintje potatoes, 14 ounces fresh cheese, 1 cup (7 ounces) thick soured cream (*crème fraîche*), 2 cloves of garlic, salt, pepper.

Peel and cut the potatoes and cook for 20 minutes in salted water with the garlic.
Finely grate the cheese.
Remove the cooked garlic and press the potatoes through a sieve to mash.
Add the soured cream and beat in the 14 ounces of grated cheese with a wooden spatula. The mixture should be perfectly smooth.
If you like, crush the second clove of raw garlic and add to the purée.

Serve very hot to the desired consistency.

PICODON

- Soft-paste cheese made from raw goat's milk, with a natural crust lightly covered in mold.
- Shape and appearance of a small cake, 3 inches in diameter and weighing about 2 ¾ ounces.
- 45% fat content.
- Area of production: Picodons are commonly found in the whole of the Rhône valley, right down to Haute-Provence. The Appellation d'origine controllée area is limited to the regions of Ardèche and Drôme and the canton of Valréas in the Vaucluse area.
- Best time: from the end of summer to the beginning of winter.

WHICH WINE?

SAINT JOSEPH
CHATEAUNEUF DU PAPE
CLAIRETTE DE DIE

These little cakes are made in very much the same manner over a huge area, although only a specific geographical zone has earned the Appellation d'origine controllée. Farmhouse and creamery produce much the same quantity. Goat's milk is first curdled, then molded and drained. Ripening continues over a period of at least twelve days, during which time the natural crust turns yellow. If left to mature longer, the crust will begin to turn blue and then reddish. When bought young, this cheese can be left to continue ripening wrapped in a vine leaf and stored in a cool cellar.

TOURNEDOS AU PICODON
Tournedos steaks with Picodon

PREPARATION TIME: 10 MINS

COOKING TIME: 10 MINS

4 Picodons, 4 very tender tournedos steaks, ½ cup (3 ½ fluid ounces) cognac, ½ cup + 2 tablespoons (5 fluid ounces) white wine, 1 knob of butter.

Melt the butter in a pan and fry the tournedos.
Deglaze the pan with the cognac and add the white wine.
Allow to reduce for a few minutes.
While the meat is cooking, put the Picodons in a buttered oven-proof dish and heat in the oven until creamy.
Arrange the tournedos on a plate and pour over the sauce. Place one soft Picodon on top of each steak.

Serve with a salad seasoned with walnut oil.

ROQUEFORT

- Firm paste, veined cheese with a thin white crust.
- Pure, whole, treated sheep's milk. It takes 4 gallons to make a Roquefort weighing 6 ½ pounds.
- 52% fat content.
- Cylinder about 8 inches in diameter and 4 inches high.
- Area of production: ripening in Roquefort only; milk collected originally from Lozère to Tarn and now also from Pyrénées-Atlantiques and Corsica.

To the south of the Massif Central mountain, in a vast land where herds of milk sheep reign, lies the little village of Roquefort-Sur-Soulzon, huddled against a massive limestone cliff dating from the Jurassic era. In the midst of these rocks are to be found the caves where centuries of Roquefort have been left to mature.
Sheep's milk is the richest of all the milks used in cheese dairies: it curdles in under two hours. This is followed by the injection of penicillium spores that give Roquefort its appetising blue veins. The cheese is then left in the silence of the caves to undergo a ripening process under biological conditions that are unique in the world.

ROULADES DE SOLE AU ROQUEFORT
Rolled sole with Roquefort

PREPARATION TIME: 10 MINS

COOKING TIME: 20 MINS

6 sole fillets, ½ cup + 1 tablespoon (4 ½ ounces) butter, 7 ounces bacon cubes, 3 ½ ounces Roquefort, 1 ¾ cups (14 fluid ounces) thick soured cream (*crème fraîche*), 6 large leaves of sorrel, 2 carrots.

Poach the sorrel leaves for 1 minute in boiling, salted water. Drain and cool under cold water. Scrape and chop the carrots. Cook in boiling water.
In a pan, fry the bacon cubes until brown. Add the cooked carrots and leave to simmer for 3 minutes. Garnish the sole fillets with this mixture.
Roll up each fillet and wrap in a sorrel leaf. Keep in place with a wooden toothpick.
Arrange the rolled fillets in an oven-proof dish, crumble over the Roquefort and cover with the soured cream. Place in a hot oven for 5 minutes.

Serve with steamed new potatoes.

WHICH WINE?

SAUTERNES
BARSAC
MONBAZILLAC

OSSAU-IRATY

- Uncooked, pressed paste with a natural, dried crust varying in color from light grey to orange-brown.
- Raw sheep's milk.
- 50% fat content.
- Wheel with a convex heel, weighing 11 pounds and up to 15 ½ pounds if farmhouse-made, with a diameter of around 12 inches.
- Area of production: Pays Basque, Béarn, Bigorre and Navarre.
- Best time: from summer to fall. Cheeses ripened on the farms reach perfection at the beginning of winter.

The beech groves of the Forest of Iraty were already known in the 18th century as a source of ships' masts for the navies of France and Spain. But since long before then it had been the home of sheep's milk cheese. Now officially known by the name Ossau-Iraty, much of the fame of this cheese is due to the processing and ripening method used. The curds are mixed with a whisk, then molded and pressed. After four months' ripening, the smooth white paste begins to take on a delicate flavor. At this point the cheese develops its unique creamy texture.

FRICASSÉE DE POULET
Chicken fricassee

PREPARATION TIME: 15 MINS

COOKING TIME: 60 MINS

1 chicken in pieces, 4 onions, 3 tomatoes, 17 ½ ounces Ossau-Iraty, 1 cup (7 fluid ounces) thick soured cream (*crème fraîche*), 3 tablespoons (1 ½ ounces) butter, 4 ¼ cups (1 ¾ pints) chicken broth, salt, pepper, thyme, bay leaves.

Remove the crust from the cheese and cut into thin strips.
Scald the tomatoes in boiling water. Cool and peel away the skins.
In a casserole dish, melt the butter and brown the chicken pieces. Add the finely chopped onions, the quartered tomatoes and the soured cream.
Moisten with the chicken broth and cook slowly for 45 minutes. When nearly ready, add the cheese and leave to melt for a few minutes over a low heat.

Serve accompanied by a gratin.

WHICH WINE?

TOKAY
CHAMPAGNE
IROULEGUY

BLEU DES CAUSSES

- Paste veined by the injection of mold with a natural crust covered in light mold.
- Raw cow's milk.
- 45% fat content.
- Cylinder measuring around 8 inches diameter and 4 inches high and weighing 6 ½ pounds.
- Area of production: Aveyron, Lot, Lozère, Gard and Hérault.
- Best time: available and sold all year round, but especially in summer and early fall. At that time, it has a very sought-after, creamy texture.

WHICH WINE?

BEAUMES DE VENISE
GEWURTZTRAMINER
POMEROL

In ancient times, flocks of sheep were moved up from the Bas-Languedoc to summer pastures in the limestone Causses and in the Aubrac mountains, where for four months they grazed side by side with the local cow herds. During this season, the milk of these cows and sheep was mixed to produce Bleu des Causses. Nowadays, only cow's milk is used for a cheese that is a very close relation of Roquefort. As with its better known cousin, the curds are injected with penicillium and then pricked with needles. Then, they are left to ripen for three months in rocky caves. During this time, the paste becomes ivory in color, with a lasting flavor.

SAUCE AU BLEU
Blue sauce

PREPARATION TIME: 10 MINS

COOKING TIME: 15 MINS

1 ¼ cups (½ pint) broth, 4 ¼ ounces Bleu des Causses, 4 tablespoons (1 ¾ ounces) butter, ½ cup (1 ¾ ounces) flour, 1 onion, 20 tarragon leaves, a sachet of mixed herbs or *bouquet garni*, ½ cup (3 ½ fluid ounces) thick soured cream (*crème fraîche*), salt, pepper.

Brown the finely chopped onion in the butter. Keep aside.
In the same pan, add the flour and stir until it turns brown. Add the broth and the cooked onion. Continue to stir, adding the mixed herbs and the pepper.
Leave to simmer over a low heat for 10 minutes, stirring constantly. Pass the sauce through a sieve.
Add the finely chopped tarragon and the Bleu cheese diced into small cubes.
Off the heat, last of all add the soured cream.
Stir to mix and serve hot in a sauce-boat.

It will provide a fine accompaniment to red meat or roast veal.

CROTTIN DE CHAVIGNOL

- Soft paste covered in a fine layer of blue or white mold.
- More than ¾ pint of goat's milk goes into a Crottin weighing 3 ounces.
- 45% fat content.
- Flat, rounded cylinder measuring about 2 inches in diameter and ¾ inches high.
- Area of production: most of the Cher and Nièvre regions and a small area of Loiret.
- Best time: from spring to the end of summer.

The picturesque little village of Chavignol in the Cher region nestles at the bottom of a hollow, between vine-covered slopes producing a delicious white wine. It has given its name to these little round cheeses, unexpectedly called Crottins *or 'little pats'.*

The curds are drained and then molded. This is followed by salting and drying, before maturing takes place in a cool cellar. There are several stages of ripeness, each corresponding to different established flavors. After two weeks' ripening the aroma begins to acquire a tang. Three months' ripening will give it piquancy. Between these two extremes it is simply a matter of individual taste.

PÂTÉ DE CHAVIGNOLS
Chavignol pie

PREPARATION TIME: 20 MINS

COOKING TIME: 105 MINS

14 ounces shortcrust pastry, 3 Crottins that are not too dry, 3 ½ ounces raw ham, 7 ounces Comté, 2 cloves of garlic, 2 egg yolks and 1 whole egg, 1 cupful of thick soured cream (*crème fraîche*), 1 ⅓ cups (9 fluid ounces) white sauce, salt, pepper.

Make the shortcrust pastry. Prepare the white sauce and when nearly ready add the cloves of garlic, the grated Comté, the soured cream and the 2 egg yolks.

Divide the shortcrust pastry into ⅔ for the base and ⅓ for the lid. Roll out and line the bottom and sides of a pie dish; the pastry should hang over the edge. Fill with alternating layers of white sauce, sliced Crottins and raw ham.

Place the lid on top and seal the edges. Make a hole in the center for the steam to escape. Beat the remaining egg lightly and brush over the top of the pie.

Bake in a hot oven for 90 minutes, then lower the temperature and continue cooking for a further 15 minutes.

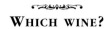

WHICH WINE?

SANCERRE
RIESLING
CÔTEAUX D'AIX

POULIGNY ST-PIERRE

- Soft paste, light-colored and creamy-textured, with a thin crust that changes color according to the degree of ripeness.
- Raw, whole goat's milk.
- 45% fat content.
- Typical, pyramid shape with a flat top, measuring 5 inches high by 4 inches along the side of the base. Weight 9 ounces.
- Extremely small area of production. It covers only the Blanc district in the Indre region.
- Best time: the flavor of this cheese is best from April to October.

The green pastures of the Brenne valley are ideal for rearing goats. This is where Pouligny Saint-Pierre is made, a cheese that is particularly enjoyable because it is produced in such small quantities. The milk undergoes the traditional phases of processing: curdling, then shaping in molds. Afterwards, the cheese is placed in a well-ventilated cooling-room, where it is left on wooden grids for the whole of the ripening period, lasting from two to five weeks. Its crust and flavor develop as it ripens; while still white, it retains a milky flavor; blue, it is faintly and very characteristically redolent of goat cheese.

CANAPÉS AU POULIGNY
Canapés with Pouligny

PREPARATION TIME: 20 MINS

1 loaf of 10-grain bread cut into slices, 3 ½ ounces very young Pouligny, ½ cup (3 ½ ounces) unsalted butter, 1 ¼ tablespoons tomatoe purée, salt, pepper.

Make a garnish with ½ cup of creamed butter, the tomatoe purée and the 3 ½ ounces of white Pouligny diced small.
Mix all the ingredients together until smooth.
Season with salt and pepper.
Spread this mixture thickly on the slices of bread.

The canapés will look even more attractive decorated with rounds of radish, tomatoes, lemon wedges or olives.

WHICH WINE?

VOUVRAY
CÔTES DU ROUSILLON

63

SELLES-SUR-CHER

- Mild tasting, soft paste cheese. The crust is tinted very slightly blue by superb molds.
- Processed from whole, raw milk.
- 45% fat content.
- Flattened cone shape weighing around 5 ounces.
- Area of production: Indre, Cher, Loir-et-Cher.
- Best time: from summer to winter.

Farmers in the areas of Sologne and the middle Cher valley in the region of Berry have been making goat's cheese for many decades. It is well known to gourmets by the name Selles-sur-Cher. The cheese is made using traditional methods. The curds are obtained by adding rennet to the milk; they are then molded by hand without breaking up, which helps to give the paste its final, meltingly creamy texture. The cheeses are then covered with a mix of crumbly charcoal and salt to help them mature during at least ten days. Alone, the cheese should be eaten without its crust.

TOMATES AU CHÈVRE
Tomatoes with goat's cheese

PREPARATION TIME: 20 MINS

4 tomatoes, 1 bunch basil, 1 goat's cheese, 2 ½ tablespoons capers, half a cucumber, 2 ½ tablespoons olive oil, pepper.

Wash the tomatoes. Using a sharp, serrated knife, slice finely leaving the slices joined at the bottom.
Carefully cut the cheese into thin slices, then cut in half again so that the slices are the same size as the tomatoes.
Spread out the cheese slices, drizzle with olive oil, sprinkle with chopped basil and season with pepper. Slide the cheese between the slices of tomato. Decorate with capers and a few slices of cucumber.

Serve chilled.

WHICH WINE?

BOURGEUIL
MONTLOUIS
CORBIÈRES

SAINTE-MAURE

The ancient province of Touraine, the origin of today's regions of Indre and Loir-et-Cher, is one of the areas with the longest history of goat's cheese production. Sainte-Maure has always been highly appreciated along the banks of the Cher and the farm dairies continue to make the cheese according to time-honoured tradition. The curds are placed in molds without draining. When the cheese is unmolded, it is left to dry and ripen for a month. Taste it without its crust to enjoy its magnificent fruity flavor.

- Soft paste with a fine, textured crust covered in white and blueish mold.
- Raw goat's milk. It takes 3 ½ pints of milk to make just one cheese.
- 45% fat content.
- Flattened-cone-shaped log, 10 inches long and weighing 9 ounces.
- Area of production: Indre-et-Loire as well as part of Loir-et-Cher and Indre.
- Best time: from spring to winter, but peak quality is reached in May and June.

ŒUFS GRATINÉS
Eggs gratin

PREPARATION TIME: 20 MINS

COOKING TIME: 30 MINS

3 ½ ounces Sainte-Maure, 5 eggs, 10 ½ ounces onions, 14 ounces tomatoes, 2 tablespoons (1 ounce) butter, 2 ½ tablespoons olive oil, 1 glass white wine, ½ cup + 2 tablespoons (5 fluid ounces) thick soured cream (*crème fraîche*), 1 clove garlic, salt, pepper.

Cooks the eggs in boiling water for 10 minutes.
Finely chop the onions and brown them slowly in the butter. After 10 minutes moisten with the white wine.
Off the heat add the soured cream.
Remove the shells from the eggs and cut in half.
Rub an oven-proof dish with the garlic and spread the onions over the bottom.
Top with the sliced tomatoes.
Place the eggs on this base and sprinkle with the crumbled cheese.

Brown under the grill for 10 minutes.

WHICH WINE?

BOURGOGNE ALIGOTÉ
CHINON BLANC
HERMITAGE

CHABICHOU

- Pale, soft paste under a white or light yellow crust covered in surface mold.
- Whole, raw goat's milk. Two versions: creamery and farmhouse. The second is more difficult to find.
- 45% fat content.
- Cylinder 2 ½ inches high and 2 ½ inches across. Net weight 5 ounces.
- Area of production: part of the regions of Vienne, Deux-Sèvres and Charente.
- Best time: can be enjoyed from June to November

The saying goes that no one who has failed to sample the nutty flavor of a Chabichou from Poitou can call themselves a true cheese lover. The cheese is made according to the traditional ritual. After curdling, it is drained and shaped in molds, then salted and placed in cold-storage for two weeks to ripen. During this time the crust develops, its colour betraying its origin. Farmhouse Chabichou grows a blue-grey surface mold, while the crust of creamery cheeses varies from white to yellow. The creamery version is successfully produced industrially using techniques based on traditional know-how.

TIAN PROVENÇAL
Provence 'tian'

PREPARATION TIME: 20 MINS

COOKING TIME: 35 MINS

4 medium sized zucchini, 4 tomatoes, 1 clove garlic, 1 young cheese, 1 ¼ tablespoons thyme, 5 tablespoons pure olive oil, 7 ounces cooked rice, salt, pepper, origano.

Cut the tomatoes and zucchini into round slices ½ inch thick.
Slice the cheese into rounds ¼ inch thick.
Peel the garlic. Crush in the oil and use this mixture to grease an oven-proof dish, clay if you have one.
Spread the rice in a layer. Cover with alternating rounds of vegetables and cheese.
Sprinkle with thyme, origano, salt and pepper.

Cook in a hot oven and serve warm.

LIST OF PHOTOGRAPHS

By the same publisher

MARIA CHIARA MARTINELLI

Al Dente

All the Secrets of Italy's
Genuine Home-Style Cooking

P/b, 10″ × 8 3/8″ (254 × 215 mm);
208 pages; 128 color photos

ISBN 88-7301-141-1 • US$ 19.95 £ 12.95

Famous, and justly so, for its artistic and cultural treasures, Italy is equally renowned for its rich gastronomic tradition, having made the world a gift of such all-time favorites as pizza and pasta.

But even if these specialties have by now become part and parcel of the cuisine of many countries – though perhaps not always in their most authentic forms – there are countless other original dishes just as typical of genuine Italian home cooking, and equally as popular in Italy, only waiting to be discovered.

Al Dente has been specially conceived and written by an Italian expert for all lovers of Italian cuisine around the world who wish to recreate the tastes and aromas of this colorful sun-drenched country in their own homes, to explore all its infinite variations. In addition to a detailed panorama of Italy's most characteristic products (from cheeses to oils, pasta to wines), and a rich supplement of the most typical dishes region by region, here are all the recipes, a complete and indispensable collection of the great 'standards' of traditional Italian cooking.

Clear and simple explanations make these recipes easy to follow, even for those with little experience in foreign cooking.

Interesting sidelights and curious facts highlight each dish, useful tips as well as substitute ingredients for products perhaps not readily available in some countries amplify each recipe.

One of the great strengths of this volume is the absolute authenti/city of the recipes proposed, many of which have been handed down for generations, untouched by the adaptations of 'compromises' introduced by standardized commercial catering. The true beauty and secret of Italian cooking is, in fact, its utter simplicity. You will surely discover this as you follow the author's explanations and good advice and see how easy it is to make Italy's culinary tradition your own, bringing its fine art to your own table in its truest, most genuine expression.